Living History

General Store

A Village Store in 1902

by Megan O'Hara
Photography by Tim Rummelhoff

Content Consultant
Charlie Pautler, Site Manager
Historic Forestville

Blue Earth Books
an imprint of Capstone Press

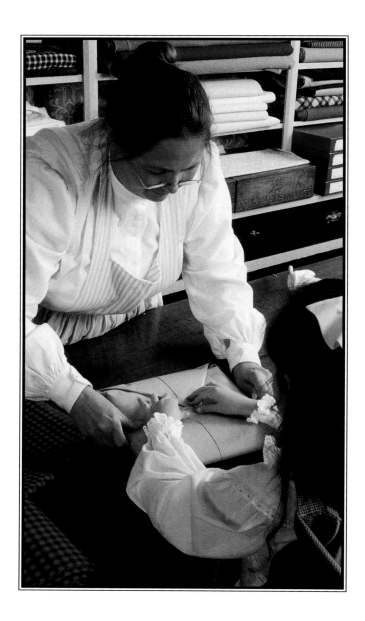

Blue Earth Books
818 North Willow Street, Mankato, Minnesota 56001
http://www.capstone-press.com

Library of Congress Cataloging-in-Publication Data
O'Hara, Megan.
    General store: a village store in 1902/by Megan O'Hara.
    p. cm.--(Living History)
    Summary: Describes the role of the general store in nineteenth
century rural America. Includes related activities.
    ISBN 1-56065-723-5
    1. General stores--United States--History--Juvenile literature. [1. General Store. 2. United
States--Social life and customs--19th century.] I. Title. II. Series:
Living History (Mankato, Minn.)
HF5429.3.043   1998
381'.1--dc21   97-31876
                                                                  CIP
                                   381.1   AC
                                   OHA

Editorial credits:
Editor, Christy Steele; design, Patricia Bickner Linder; illustrations, Timothy Halldin

Photo credits:
Michelle Coughlan, 17
Minnesota Historical Society, 27 (top), 28
All other photographs by Tim Rummelhoff

Contents

Introduction 5

Meighen Store, 1902 8

Trading Eggs 12

Barter and Credit 16

The Smell of Coffee Beans 19

Cloth 21

Picking Up the Mail 25

Saying Good-bye 27

Activities

Make Apple Butter 17

Family Circulars 25

Features

Words to Know 30

To Learn More 30

Internet Sites 30

Places to Write and Visit 31

About the General Store at Historic Forestville 32

Acknowledgments

We are grateful to the following for contributing their time, knowledge, and expertise: Charles Pautler, site manager, Historic Forestville; Sandy Scheevel, site technician; Liz Turchin, Laurie Brickley, and Michael Cook of the Minnesota Historical Society; interpreters Sandy Scheevel and George Colbenson; and volunteer Devon McGrane. We are also grateful for the use of this Minnesota Historical Society site and artifacts to recreate life at a village general store.

Location of Meighen Store at Historic Forestville Near Preston, Minnesota

Meighen Store

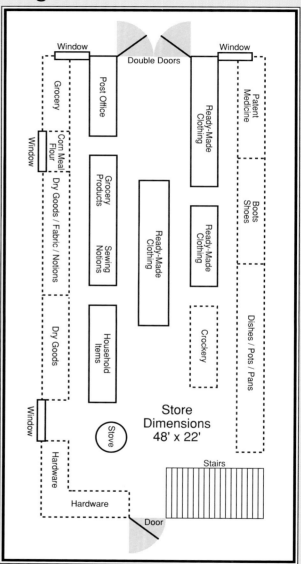

Introduction

In the early 1900s, people in small farm communities bought most of their supplies from general stores. These stores sold nearly anything. General stores sold rakes and hoes for gardening. They sold glass jars for storing berries, fruits, and vegetables. They sold cloth and thread to make clothes.

General stores sold special foods. Farmers also bought some basic foods like salt, sugar, and flour there.

Farm families made many things by hand. They often made soap and clothes. General stores sold the supplies that families needed to make these things.

People sometimes wanted to buy things they could not make themselves. They told the storekeeper what they wanted. The storekeeper ordered these items from suppliers in large cities.

The storekeeper was an important person in the community.

The storekeeper knew all the customers. A customer is a person who buys something from a store. The storekeeper made sure customers had the supplies they needed.

Farmers grew crops and then sold the crops for money. Farm families might not have much money while the crops were growing. The storekeeper sometimes let people trade eggs, chickens, or other goods. In return, they received things from the store. This was called bartering. Other times, the storekeeper let people buy things on credit. The storekeeper wrote down people's purchases in an account book. People paid their accounts after they received money for their crops or animals.

In many places, the storekeeper was also the community's postmaster. The storekeeper was in charge of sending, receiving, and handing out mail.

The general store was a popular place. Life on a farm was lonely at times. People knew they would see neighbors and friends when they came to the store. A trip to the store was an exciting event.

Meighen Store was the general store in the village of Forestville. Farm families traveled long distances to shop at the store. This book tells the story of what a trip to Meighen Store may have been like.

GENERAL STORE

Someday I'm going to have a store
With tinkly bells hung over the door,
With real glass cases and counters wide
And drawers all spilly with things inside.
There'll be a little of everything:
Bolts of calico, balls of string;
Jars of peppermint, tins of tea,
Potatoes and kettles and crockery;

Seeds in packets, scissors bright;
Kegs of sugar, brown and white;
Sarsaparilla for picnic lunches;
Bananas and rubber boots in bunches.
I'll fix the window and dust each shelf,
And take the money in all myself.
It will be my store and I will say:
"What can I do for you today?"

Rachel Field

Meighen Store, 1902

My name is Margaret Murphy. I am nearly nine years old. Father brought me to town in the wagon today. I am going to Meighen Store while he visits the blacksmith. The blacksmith is going to make a new shoe for our horse.

Mother usually does the shopping. Today, it is my job. Mother gave me a list of things that I must buy. She stayed home with my baby brother Michael. Mother is worried about Michael because he has whooping cough.

Whooping Cough

In the early 1900s, whooping cough was a common disease. It mostly affected children. The disease often killed newborn babies.

The disease begins like a cold. People have runny noses and begin coughing. After about two weeks, the coughing becomes so bad that people gasp for air. The noise they make sounds like a whoop. This noise gave whooping cough its name.

It takes six to 10 weeks to recover from whooping cough. Today, people get shots to protect them from this disease. In the past, there were no shots. Whooping cough often caused pneumonia, convulsions, brain damage, or death.

The storekeeper is Mr. Thomas Meighen. Mr. Meighen knows the farmers and their families by name. He knows my name, too. Sometimes he gives me a piece of candy from the candy jars on the counter. He wraps the sweets in wax paper to keep them fresh. Licorice is my favorite. Maybe he will give me a piece today.

The store sells many wonderful things, but it does not have everything. Once Father wanted to buy windows for our house. Mr. Meighen did not have any, so he ordered them from a store in the city. They sent the windows to us in barrels filled with sawdust. The sawdust kept the windows from breaking. It took three months for the windows to get here.

Trading Eggs

Mother often brings eggs, butter, or cream to the general store. We trade these items for supplies we need. Today, I am in charge of trading our eggs. I know this is a good batch of eggs. They are large and fresh. None of them are cracked.

I was very careful with the eggs on the way to the store. I put the eggs in a basket and packed straw around them. This kept them from breaking during the wagon ride. The road to town is made of dirt. The wagon bumps a lot when we drive over it.

First I will trade the eggs. Then I will put our goods in the empty basket. I hope everything on Mother's list will fit in the basket.

Mr. Meighen must decide what price he will pay for our eggs. He studies each egg closely. He candles the eggs to make sure they are good. To do this, he lights a candle. He holds each egg in front of the flame. The candle's light lets him see whether the egg is fresh or whether the yolks have spoiled.

Spoiled Food

Keeping food from spoiling was a big problem for storekeepers in the early 1900s. There were no refrigerators to keep things cool and fresh.

Today, the government tests products to make sure they are fresh. Back then, there were no government tests. People often bought spoiled food. There were sometimes insects in the food. Crackers might be broken and dirty. Butter could be runny. People could die or become sick from eating these spoiled foods.

Storekeepers tried to keep food fresh. They dried meat in the sun or soaked it in vinegar. The meat tasted different, but it stayed fresh longer. Storekeepers put other foods in root cellars. A root cellar is a cool, underground room. Cool temperatures helped goods like vegetables and fruits stay fresh.

A Fair Barter

The barter system was a way of trading goods for other goods. It was not perfect. Sometimes customers with high-quality goods got the same amount as those with bad goods. For example, some people bartered sour, lumpy apple butter. They might have received the same amount of money as those who bartered sweet, smooth apple butter.

Some storekeepers gave those with better goods more credit than those with bad goods. This could cause hurt feelings. People sometimes felt the storekeeper was being unfair.

Not all storekeepers were honest. Some tried to cheat their customers. They added sawdust to oatmeal. They painted ordinary beans black to look like coffee beans.

Some farmers tried to cheat storekeepers. They tried to barter spoiled goods.

But the barter system worked well most of the time. It helped farm families with little money survive.

Barter and Credit

Mr. Meighen says that our eggs are worth 25 cents. This is a good price for the eggs. He writes this amount in his account book. Now I can get other supplies with the egg money.

Our family does not have much money. We trade farm goods for store goods. We agree on a fair trade. This is called bartering.

Mr. Meighen lets us buy on credit if we do not have goods to barter. He writes the amount of money we owe in his book. We pay him back when we sell our crops or farm animals.

Make Apple Butter

Sometimes farm families made goods like butter or jelly to trade at the general store. Apple butter was a favorite type of food to barter. Ask an adult to help you make your own apple butter.

What You Need

6 large apples

1 cup (.24 liter) water

1 tablespoon (15 milliliters) cinnamon

1/8 teaspoon (.63 milliliter) cloves

1/4 cup plus 2 tablespoons (.06 liter plus 30 milliliters) frozen apple-juice concentrate

1 tablespoon (15 milliliters) cornstarch

What You Do

1. Peel and core the apples. Then cut the apples into thin slices.
2. Put the water and 1/4 cup (.06 liter) of frozen apple-juice concentrate in a pan. Add the cinnamon and cloves. Mix in the apple slices.
3. Put the pan on the stove. Bring the mixture to a boil.
4. Reduce the heat. Simmer the mixture for one hour.
5. In a separate bowl, mix the cornstarch with the remaining two tablespoons (30 milliliters) of apple juice.
6. Add the cornstarch mixture to the pan. Cook it for several minutes until the mixture thickens.
7. Pour the mixture into a blender and blend until it is smooth.

You now have your own apple butter. You can spread it on bread, pancakes, or crackers.

The Smell of Coffee Beans

The coffee smell in the general store reminds me of cozy mornings by the kitchen stove. Coffee is one of Mother's favorite drinks. She likes to drink one cup every morning.

Mother wants me to buy one pound (.45 kilograms) of coffee. Mr. Meighen carefully weighs the coffee beans on his scale.

Cloth

Mrs. Meighen helps Mr. Meighen run the
store. She buys the fabrics. She stocks fine
dress goods. There are handsome
flannels and colorful calicos.
There are challis fabrics,
too. Challis is soft
and smooth.

I love the clean smell of the bolts of cloth. Mother has ordered some checked flannel. It is very soft. She will make some flannel shirts and dresses for us. We will wear them this winter.

The store also sells decorations for the fabric. Lace, ribbons, and braid will make a fancy dress for someone. I love to touch the soft, slippery ribbons. Soon I will learn how to sew.

Picking Up the Mail

We pick up our mail at Meighen Store. Mr. Meighen puts the mail in our mail slot. It is always exciting to get mail. We are expecting the family circular to arrive soon. Mother wants to read the news from Aunt Katie. Aunt Katie lived with us on the farm until she moved to Boston. She is a teacher now. We all miss her.

Mr. Meighen hands me the mail. Under Father's newspaper is the family circular. Aunt Katie has written! Mother will open the letter and read it to the whole family tonight. Father will be happy to read the newspaper.

Family Circulars

Family members often moved to distant places. They had trouble staying in contact. Few people had telephones.

Some people started family circulars. At the beginning of each month, one family member started the circular. This person took a piece of paper and wrote news from his or her life.

This person mailed the paper to a cousin, a sister, or another family member. Then the family member mailed the circular to somebody else until all family members had added news.

The last family member mailed the circular to the person who began it. This person collected the circulars. Family circulars served as a family history.

You can start your own family circular. Take some paper and write a little about your life. Send this to one of your family members and ask him or her to add news. Have this family member mail it to another family member.

Collect the family circular after every family member has written news. You can start a family circular as often as you like. Put the circulars in a folder and read them whenever you want. The circulars can serve as your family's history.

Saying Good-bye

I am almost ready to leave. Other customers come in and out of the store. Each one greets Mr. and Mrs. Meighen. I see my neighbors and talk to them for awhile. I see more people in one hour at the store than I do all month on our farm.

Mr. Meighen takes a break to play a game of checkers with a farmer. Mrs. Marty is also resting on the store's porch. She says she hopes my brother gets better. I thank her for thinking of us.

It is time to meet Father by the wagon. I say goodbye
to Mr. and Mrs. Meighen. Mother will be pleased to see
the mail and the goods I have purchased. I hope she will
send me to shop at Meighen Store again soon.

Words to Know

barter (BAR-tur)—a system of exchanging goods for other goods

blacksmith (BLAK-smith)—someone who makes and fits horseshoes

bolt (BOHLT)—a roll of cloth

calico (KAL-i-koh)—cotton cloth printed with a colorful pattern

challis (SHA-lee)—a lightweight, soft fabric made of cotton, wool, or yarns

convulsion (kuhn-VUL-shuhn)—an uncontrollable jerking of the muscles

credit (KRED-it)—to buy something and pay for it later

flannel (FLAN-uhl)—a soft, woven cloth made of cotton or wool

postmaster (POHST-mass-tur)—the head of a post office

root cellar (ROOT SEL-ur)—a cool, underground room

To Learn More

Kalman, Bobbie. *The General Store*. New York: Crabtree Publishing, 1997.

Kalman, Bobbie. *19th Century Clothing*. New York: Crabtree Publishing, 1993.

Kalman, Bobbie and David Schimpky. *Old-time Toys*. New York: Crabtree Publishing, 1995.

O'Hara, Megan. *Pioneer Farm: A Farm on the Prairie in the 1880s*. Mankato, Minn.: Blue Earth Books, 1998.

Internet Sites

Conner Prairie
http://www.connerprairie.org/cp/home.html

Living History Resources
http://history1700s.miningco.com/msub5.htm

Minnesota Historical Society
http://www.mnhs.org/index.html

Welcome to the General Store
http://www.hfmgv.org/gs/gs-front.html

Places to Write and Visit

California
San Gregorio General Store
7615 Stage Road
San Gregorio, CA 94074

Connecticut
Mystic Seaport Museum
75 Greenmanville Avenue
Mystic, CT 06355

Illinois
Lincoln's New Salem
Route 97
Petersburg, IL 62675

Naper Settlement Museum
201 West Porter Avenue
Naperville, IL 60540-6525

Indiana
Conner Prairie Pioneer Settlement
13400 Allisonville Road
Fishers, IN 46038-4499

Iowa
1875 Town of Walnut Hill
2600 NW 111th Street
Urbandale, IA 50322

Massachusetts
Old Sturbridge Village
Route 20
Sturbridge, MA 01566

Michigan
Greenfield Village
20900 Oakwood Boulevard
P.O. Box 1970
Dearborn, MI 48121-1970

Minnesota
Harkin Store
Brown County Historical Society
2 North Broadway
New Ulm, MN 56073

Historic Forestville
RR 2, P.O. Box 126
Preston, MN 55965

Nebraska
Pioneer Village
P. O. Box 68
Minden, NE 68959

New Hampshire
Dunaway Store
P.O. Box 300
Portsmouth, NH 03802

Poulsen's General Store
1000 Monroe Road
Littleton, NH 03561

Vermont
Vermont Country Store
Route 100
Weston, VT 05161

Virginia
Colonial Williamsburg
P.O. Box 3585
Williamsburg, VA 23187

Ontario, Canada
Doon Heritage Crossroads
RR 2
Kitchener, ON   N2G 3W5
Canada

About the General Store at Historic Forestville

Meighen Store is located in southeastern Minnesota. It was once owned by Mr. and Mrs. Meighen and located in Forestville, a small village much like those found in many 1850s farming regions. By the 1860s, 100 people lived in Forestville. The town had 20 buildings, including two general stores, a grist mill, a brickyard, two hotels, and a school. Forestville grew until the railroad bypassed the community in 1868. Village residents watched their town struggle to survive while towns served by the railroad continued to grow.

Today the general store, the family home, a granary, a barn, and a wagon barn are all that remain of Forestville. The site is operated by the Minnesota Historical Society and is open to visitors during the summer. Costumed interpreters perform the activities of daily life in 1899. For more information, call the Minnesota Historical Society at 507-765-2785 or visit the society's Internet site at <http://www.mnhs.org>.